A FLEA for JUSTICE

Marian Wright Edelman Stands Up for Change

VALERIE BOLLING

Illustrated by
TEMIKA GROOMS

Charlesbridge

Marian Wright Edelman is a flea for justice.

Do you want to know what a flea has to do with justice?

Well, it all started during a time when there were laws that said Black people and white people had to be separated. Four-year-old Marian wasn't thinking about those laws when she took a drink from the nearest water fountain. She felt a hand on her shoulder, yanking her away.

Her Sunday school teacher pointed to the sign. Marian didn't understand, and she didn't like being told she couldn't do something.

"The outside world was there telling us we were not equal and not worth anything."

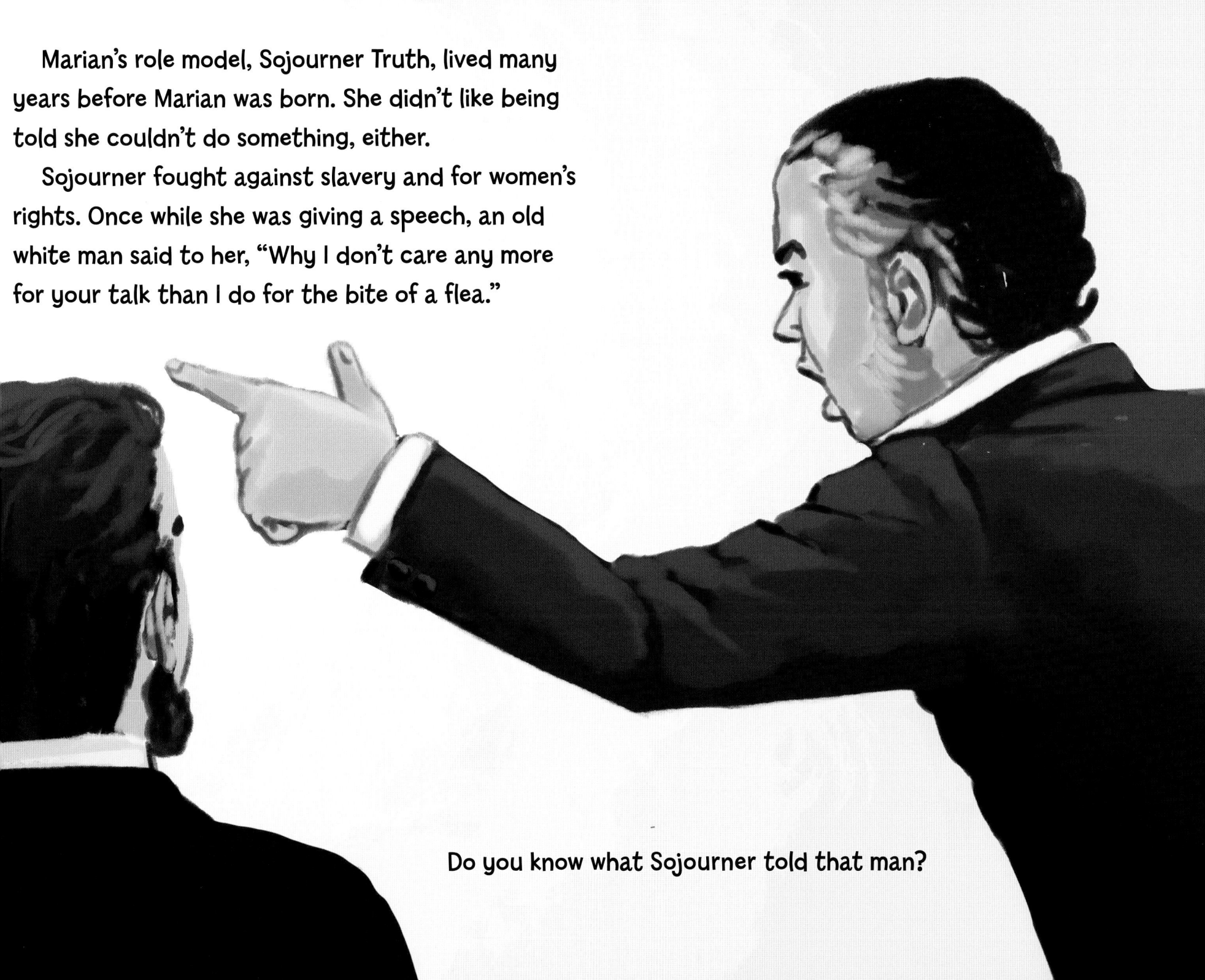

Marian's role model, Sojourner Truth, lived many years before Marian was born. She didn't like being told she couldn't do something, either.

Sojourner fought against slavery and for women's rights. Once while she was giving a speech, an old white man said to her, "Why I don't care any more for your talk than I do for the bite of a flea."

Do you know what Sojourner told that man?

She said, "Perhaps not, but Lord willing,
I'll keep you scratching."

Sojourner promised to make that man—and everyone
else—scratch until slavery was abolished.

She was a flea for justice! And Marian was one, too!

"I was a Black kid who wanted to be useful . . .

COLORED

Marian switched those water fountain signs every chance she got.

and I wanted to change things.
I was raised to change things."

WHITE

If white folks knew they were drinking water meant for Black people, that certainly would've made them scratch!

The signs needed to go. And other things needed to change, too.

Marian and her Black classmates had to read hand-me-down books from a white school. She didn't like that.

Marian witnessed a car accident, and the white policemen wouldn't help the injured Black people. She knew that wasn't right.

Marian's friend died after stepping on a rusty nail, because the hospital refused to treat him because he was Black. She wanted incidents like this to stop happening.

She wanted to make people scratch.

Marian couldn't fix those problems as easily as she could change the signs above water fountains. But as she got older, she found more and more ways to be a flea.

Want to know how Marian did that?

She and other college students refused to leave their seats at restaurants that wouldn't serve Black people.

Marian became the first Black woman lawyer in Mississippi. She defended people who were arrested for helping Black people register to vote.

And Marian marched with Reverend Dr. Martin Luther King Jr. and thousands of others for Black people's equal rights.

"If we don't stand up for children, then we don't stand for much."

When Dr. King was killed, Marian lost a dear friend. She knew his death left people of all ages heartbroken, including schoolchildren. Some were sad. Some were angry. Others wanted to hurt people.

You know what Marian told them?

She said they shouldn't throw away their future by using violence.

A boy said to her, "Lady, what future? I ain't got no future. I ain't got nothing to lose."

As a child, Marian switched signs. What could she change now to make sure this boy and all children had a future?

"I've been trying to prove that boy's truth wrong . . ."

How could Marian bite and make people scratch in a big way?

Marian's father's words rang in her ears, "Get your education.
Get your education."

That was it! Marian could make sure children received a
good education and became smarter. Smart people make
others scratch until things change for the better.

"Education is for improving the lives of others and for leaving your community and world better than you found it."

How do you think Marian helped children become smarter?

She started an organization called the Children's Defense Fund. She also created Freedom Schools so children could continue to learn during the summer.

Reading is a part of everything Freedom Schools students do. Marian's father had made sure she had books at home even before she got new shoes. So students get a brand-new book every week.

CLEAN YOUR ROOM, HARVEY MOON! by PAT CUMMINGS

"What we need is for each of us to be a strategic flea for justice.

They also have fun with motivational cheers and chants. Every day students sing, and they shout "Harambee!" which means "Let's pull together!"

And they learn how to be fleas for justice. A swarm of fleas!

Enough fleas biting can make the very biggest dog uncomfortable."

Today anyone can drink from whatever water fountain they want. But people still need to stand up for more change. Everyone can be a flea for justice.
Just like Sojourner and Marian.

"If you don't like the way the world is, you change it. You have an obligation to change it. You just do it one step at a time."

What will you do to make someone scratch?

Significant Years in Marian's Life

1939: Born in Bennettsville, South Carolina, on June 6.

1953: Father dies when Marian is fourteen.

1956: Graduates from Marlboro Training High School in Bennettsville, South Carolina.

1959: Becomes involved in the Civil Rights Movement.

1960: Is arrested along with seventy-seven other students during a sit-in.
Graduates later that year as valedictorian of Spelman College.

1963: Graduates from Yale Law School in New Haven, Connecticut.

1964: Becomes the first African American woman admitted to the Mississippi Bar.
Works on racial justice issues during the Mississippi Freedom Summer and helps create the Head Start program, which offers early childhood education for children in need.

1968: Moves to Washington, DC, and helps organize Reverend Dr. Martin Luther King Jr.'s Poor People's Campaign and the Southern Christian Leadership Conference.

1968: Marries Peter Edelman.

1973: Starts the Children's Defense Fund.

1985: Receives a MacArthur Fellowship, an honor that comes with funds to convey a belief in one's work and potential.

1987: Publishes her first book, *Families in Peril: An Agenda for Social Change.*

1988: Wins an Albert Schweitzer Prize for Humanitarianism for her work and exceptional contributions to humanity.

1993: Launches Children's Defense Fund Freedom Schools, modeled after temporary Freedom Schools created by the Student Nonviolent Coordinating Committee (SNCC) in 1964.

2000: Receives the Presidential Medal of Freedom, the United States' highest civilian award.

2020: Retires and becomes President Emerita of the Children's Defense Fund.

More About Marian

When Marian was a child, Black people didn't have the same rights as white people. They couldn't eat at the same restaurants, use the same public bathrooms, or drink from the same water fountains. Many places were labeled with signs that said "White" or "Colored." Today, instead of "colored," we use terms such as "Black," "African American," "of African descent," or "BIPOC" (Black, Indigenous, and People of Color), depending how people identify.

In the South, where Marian lived, Black and white children couldn't go to the same schools. The schools for Black children were run-down, had old furniture, and didn't have new books. Still, Marian was an excellent student.

"I was raised to change things."

After graduating from college, she volunteered at the National Association for the Advancement of Colored People (NAACP). Poor people and Black people couldn't get lawyers because white lawyers wouldn't take them as clients. This experience, as well as the injustices Marian witnessed throughout her life, motivated her to go to law school. Despite the challenges at Yale Law School, Marian stuck with it. She knew a law degree could help her carry out the work she felt called to do.

Marian became the first Black woman lawyer in Mississippi. In court she defended Freedom Summer activists who were arrested for helping Black people register to vote. Marian was involved in the Southern Christian Leadership Conference, the Student Nonviolent Coordinating Committee, and worked closely with Reverend Dr. Martin Luther King Jr.

She helped establish the Head Start program and later founded the Children's Defense Fund, serving as its president for forty-five years. The Children's Defense Fund continues to be a voice for poor children, children of color, and children with disabilities. Marian believes that "As adults we are responsible for meeting the needs of children. It is our moral obligation."

Marian has been an activist—a flea for justice—throughout her life. She has received more than one hundred honorary degrees and many awards, including the Presidential Medal of Freedom and the American Bar Association's Thurgood Marshall Award.

Marian and her husband, Peter, have three children, Joshua, Jonah, and Ezra; two granddaughters, Ellika and Zoe; and two grandsons, Elijah and Levi.

Author's Note

When I decided to write a picture book about Marian Wright Edelman, I immediately thought about my dear friend Victor Kuo. When we graduated from Teachers College, Columbia University, he introduced me to Mrs. Edelman's work by giving me her book *The Measure of Our Success: A Letter to My Children and Yours.*

I revisited the book on my shelf and read the beautiful inscription Victor had written. He wrote, in part: "To one who continues along an unfettered line of African American women." I reached out to him even though we hadn't communicated in almost three decades. I sadly discovered that he had recently passed away. I also learned that Victor had led a life similar to Mrs. Edelman's—a life of service to young people.

Mrs. Edelman once said, "Education was always there, but it was always education to give back and to leave the world better." And Victor once wrote, "Adolescents of whatever background are capable of achieving their goals given the proper direction and opportunity; the greatest opportunity we have to offer is education."

Like Victor and Mrs. Edelman, I am a champion for all children . . . and a flea for justice.

Learn More

Alexander, Kwame, and Kadir Nelson. *The Undefeated*. Boston, MA: Versify, 2019.

Bandy, Michael S., Eric Stein, and James E. Ransome. *Granddaddy's Turn: A Journey to the Ballot Box*. Somerville, MA: Candlewick Press, 2015.

Bolling, Valerie, Kailei Pew, and Laylie Frazier. *I See Color*. New York: Harper Collins, 2024.

Langley, Sharon, Amy Nathan, and Floyd Cooper. *A Ride to Remember: A Civil Rights Story*. New York: Abrams Books for Young Readers, 2020.

Littlesugar, Amy, and Floyd Cooper. *Freedom School, Yes!* New York: Philomel Books, 2001.

Pinkney, Andrea Davis, and Brian Pinkney. *Sojourner Truth's Step-Stomp Stride*. New York: Disney / Jump at the Sun, 2009.

Weatherford, Carole Boston, and Jerome Lagarrigue. *Freedom on the Menu: The Greensboro Sit-Ins*. New York: Puffin, 2007.

Source Notes

Main Text

"The outside world . . . worth anything": Schatz, Howard. "Above and Beyond with Marian Wright Edelman." *On Seeing Journal*, September 17, 2019. www.howardschatz.com/on-seeing-a-journal-above-and-beyond-marian-wright-edelman-founder-childrens-defense-fund.

"Why I don't care . . . bite of a flea": Edelman, Marian Wright. *The Measure of Our Success: A Letter to My Children and Yours.* New York: Harper Perennial, 1992, pp. 59–60.

"Perhaps not . . . scratching": Edelman, Marian Wright. *The Measure of Our Success*, p. 60.

"I was a Black kid . . . change things": Blackside, Inc. "Eyes on the Prize II: Interview with Marian Wright Edelman." Washington University in St. Louis, December 19, 1988. http://repository.wustl.edu/concern/videos/6d570197t.

"If we don't stand up . . . for much": Verified in an email to the author on May 30, 2023, by the Office of the Founder at the Children's Defense Fund.

"I've been . . . truth wrong": National Association of Independent Schools (NAIS). "Marian Wright Edelman Advocating for Children." YouTube video, 2:12. July 31, 2019. www.youtube.com/watch?app=desktop&v=h7MKmTSj7HU&t.

"Lady . . . to lose": National Association of Independent Schools (NAIS). "Marian Wright Edelman Advocating for Children."

"Education is for . . . found it": Verified in an email to the author on May 30, 2023, by the Office of the Founder at the Children's Defense Fund.

"Get your education": The History Makers, "Marian Wright Edelman Details Her Father's Death." Digital Archives, Session 1, Tape 2, interviewed by Julieanna L. Richardson, April 24, 2001.

"What we need . . . dog uncomfortable": Tulane University. "Tulane 2001 Commencement Address—Marian Wright Edelman." YouTube video, 20:46. May 19, 2001. www.youtube.com/watch?v=A4Wo7dc3PH0.

"If you don't like . . . at a time": Verified in an email to the author on May 30, 2023, by the Office of the Founder at the Children's Defense Fund.

Back Matter

"As adults . . . moral obligation": Edelman, Marian Wright. *Families in Peril: An Agenda for Social Change.* Cambridge, MA: Harvard University Press, 1987, p. 30.

"Education was always . . . better": The History Makers, "Marian Wright Edelman Describes Her Parents' Educational Influence." Digital Archives, Session 1, Tape 1, Story 9, interviewed by Julieanna L. Richardson, April 24, 2001.

"Adolescents . . . offer is education": Kuo, Victor. Personal admissions essay for Teachers College, Columbia University, 1991.

Dedication

"Children . . . protect them all": Edelman, Marian Wright. "Marian Wright Edelman: Disability Rights in Black 2020." National Disability Rights Network, February 24, 2020. www.ndrn.org/resource/drib2020-marian-wright-edelman.

Selected Bibliography

Children's Defense Fund. "CDF Freedom Schools Harambee." YouTube video, 6:52. May 24, 2013. www.youtube.com/watch?v=bg3ybjJdaLY&feature=emb_logo.

Children's Defense Fund. www.childrensdefense.org.

Wide Iris. "Marian Wright Edelman." Vimeo video, 6:08. December 2, 2011. www.vimeo.com/33060667.

Children's Defense Fund. "The Talk—Marian Wright Edelman on Children Poverty in America." YouTube video, 5:01. Mar. 22, 2011. www.youtube.com/watch?v=Ehsfnztr4Qc.

In memory of my beloved friend Victor Kuo, who led a life of service
of which Marian would be proud, and for my mentor and
dear friend Kelly Starling Lyons, who encouraged me to write this story.
And, of course, for children. As Marian Wright Edelman said,
"Children—*all* children—are precious gifts. Let's love, respect and
act now to protect them all."—V. B.

Many thanks to the Brown Bookshelf, the Highlights Foundation, and
the sponsors who supported a talented group of creatives through the
Amplify Black Stories program. This book is dedicated to our future leaders
who already have a seed of change planted within them. Nurture and grow
your vision. Be brave as you reshape our beautiful world.—T. G.

Text copyright © 2025 by Valerie Bolling
Illustrations copyright © 2025 by TeMika Grooms

All rights reserved, including the right of reproduction in
whole or in part in any form. Charlesbridge and colophon are
registered trademarks of Charlesbridge Publishing, Inc.

At publication, all URLs in this book were accurate.
Charlesbridge, the author, and the illustrator are not
responsible for the content of any website.

Charlesbridge • 9 Galen Street, Watertown, MA 02472
www.charlesbridge.com

Printed in China • OPIC
(hc) 10 9 8 7 6 5 4 3 2 1

Illustrations created with digital illustration brushes
    in Adobe Photoshop
Text type set in Billy by David Buck
Edited by Karen Boss
Designed by Cathleen Schaad
Production supervised by Jennifer Most Delaney

Library of Congress Cataloging-in-Publication Data
Names: Bolling, Valerie, author. | Grooms, TeMika, illustrator.
Title: A flea for justice: Marian Wright Edelman stands up for change /
    Valerie Bolling; illustrated by TeMika Grooms.
Other titles: Marian Wright Edelman stands up for change
Description: Watertown, MA: Charlesbridge, [2025] | Includes
    bibliographical references.| Audience: Ages 6–9 | Audience:
    Grades 2–3 | Summary: "Marian Wright Edelman was a lifelong flea
    for justice—making people itch—as she pushed for racial equality."
    —Provided by publisher.
Identifiers: LCCN 2024031436 (print) | LCCN 2024031437 (ebook) |
    ISBN 9781623545826 (hardcover) | ISBN 9781632894533 (ebook)
Subjects: LCSH: Edelman, Marian Wright—Juvenile literature. | African
    American women civil rights workers—Biography—Juvenile literature. |
    African American civil rights workers—Biography—Juvenile literature. |
    African American women—Biography—Juvenile literature. | African
    Americans—Biography—Juvenile literature. | African Americans—
    Civil rights—History—20th century. | United States—Race relations—
    History—20th century.
Classification: LCC E185.97.E33 B65 2025 (print) | LCC E185.97.E33 (ebook) |
    DDC 323.092 [B]—dc23/eng/20241118
LC record available at https://lccn.loc.gov/2024031436
LC ebook record available at https://lccn.loc.gov/2024031437